A
HISTORY
OF
Film

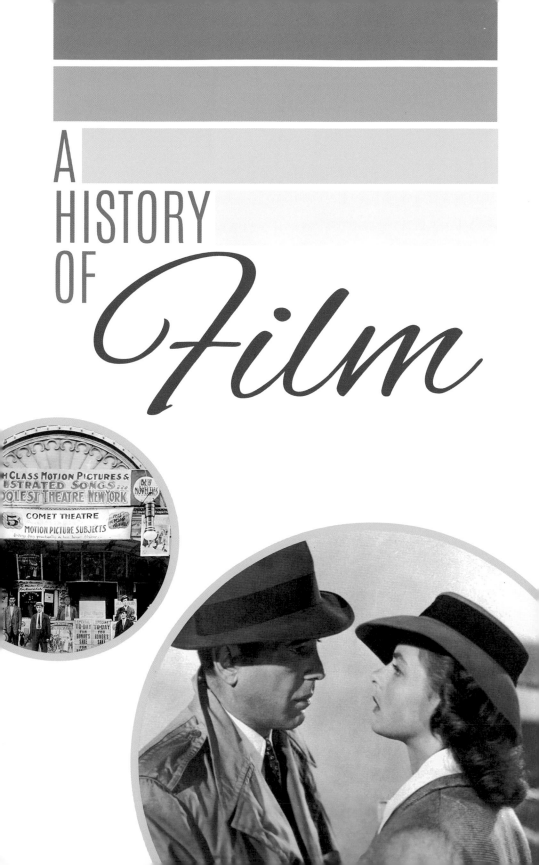

ESSENTIAL LIBRARY OF CULTURAL HISTORY

A HISTORY OF *Film*

by M. M. Eboch

Content Consultant

Kristen Hatch

Assistant Professor, Department of Film & Media Studies

Visual Studies Program, University of California, Irvine

An Imprint of Abdo Publishing | www.abdopublishing.com

www.abdopublishing.com

Published by Abdo Publishing, a division of ABDO, PO Box 398166, Minneapolis, Minnesota 55439. Copyright © 2015 by Abdo Consulting Group, Inc. International copyrights reserved in all countries. No part of this book may be reproduced in any form without written permission from the publisher. Essential Library™ is a trademark and logo of Abdo Publishing.

Printed in the United States of America, North Mankato, Minnesota
102014
012015

THIS BOOK CONTAINS
RECYCLED MATERIALS

Cover Photo: Purestock/Thinkstock
Interior Photos: Public Domain, 1 (left), 25; dapd/AP Images, 1 (right), 50; 20th Century-Fox Film Corporation/AP Images, 3 (top), 74; AP Images, 3 (bottom), 65, 61; Julien's Auctions/Rex Features/AP Images, 7; iStock/Thinkstock, 9; Thinkstock, 11; Library of Congress, 13, 31, 98, 99; Photofest NYC, 19, 23, 42, 49; Bettmann/Corbis, 28, 35, 40, 56; Harris Lewine Collection/AP Images, 32; RKO Radio Pictures/Photofest, 46; Sotheby's/Rex Features/AP Images, 58 (top); United Artists/Photofest, 58 (bottom); Rex USA/Rex Features, 59; Columbia Pictures/Photofest, 67; Everett Collection, 69; Wally Fong/AP Images, 72; FeatureFlash/Shutterstock Images, 75; Steve Schapiro/Corbis, 81; MCA/Universal Pictures/Photofest, 85; Buena Vista Distribution Company/Photofest, 89; Warner Bros./Photofest, 92, 97, 101

Editor: Melissa York
Series Designer: Maggie Villaume

Library of Congress Control Number: 2014943861

Cataloging-in-Publication Data

Eboch, M.M.
 A history of film / M.M. Eboch.
  p. cm. -- (Essential library of cultural history)
 ISBN 978-1-62403-554-8 (lib. bdg.)
 Includes bibliographical references and index.
 1. Motion pictures--History--Juvenile literature.   I. Title.
 791.4309--dc23

                                                         2014943861

CONTENTS

Chapter 1

An American Art Form

$\mathcal{I}$n the long history of art and culture, the art of making motion pictures is a relative infant. The first use of "moving pictures" dates back to the 1500s, but true movies, as we think of them today, are little more than a century old. Yet in that time, film has become a major industry employing thousands of people. It is one of the most accessible art forms, entertaining millions every week.

The history of cinema is closely tied to the development of technology. Capturing moving pictures, projecting them, adding sound, and transitioning to color all required technological breakthroughs.

The history of film is a story of the imagination and the human experience.

At first, the flashy effects of new technology were enough to capture the public's interest. In the early 1900s, people would line up to see a film depicting a few seconds of daily activity. Soon filmmakers and writers added and developed elements of story. Movies tapped into every literary genre, from comedy to fantasy to horror. Animation and special effects have their own histories running parallel to standard live-action pictures.

Going Hollywood

Film has its roots in Europe and the United States. From 1914 to 1918, World War I disrupted the industry in Europe, allowing Hollywood, California, in the United States to dominate. Many aspects of filmmaking are still centered in Hollywood, though today many films are shot on location around the world.

In recent decades, new systems have allowed people to watch movies in their homes. While this cut into cinema visits, it also created a huge secondary market for home video and, recently, streaming movies. A film now has a life long after it plays in the theater.

Although home movie cameras existed fairly early, it took decades for higher quality, cheaper cameras to

become widely available. Recently, digital media that is cheaper than traditional film has become common. These changes have allowed ordinary people to make movies on their own. Some independent filmmakers have begun achieving low-budget success. Making movies is now accessible to everyone.

Film is a technology, a business, a form of entertainment, and an art form. Its influence has spread throughout culture and society. People quote lines from films and gossip about movie stars. Movies can get people talking, whether it is a discussion of serious issues or enthusiasm about special effects. American films are known around the world. While cinema has gone global, the United States, and Hollywood in particular, is still seen as the center of moviemaking. In many ways, cinema can be considered a particularly American art form.

Chapter 2

Moving Pictures

*P*eople have projected images onto screens for centuries. In Asia, shadow puppets have been popular for 1,000 years. The shadows of figures are cast onto a screen of white fabric. A puppeteer manipulates the puppets on one side of the screen, which is in front of a light source. The audience sits on the other side of the screen. Shadow-puppet shows were used both for ceremonies and popular entertainment.

In the 1600s, inventors in the Netherlands used a lens to project images onto a wall. They used the sun or a candle as a light source. Soon after, a device called a magic lantern combined the light source, lens, and image into one portable machine. The magic lantern

The earliest projected images were shadow puppets.

grew more complex over the next two centuries. One performer mounted his lantern on wheels. He could shift it while adjusting the lens to maintain focus. A shutter allowed him to dissolve one image into another. He developed shows featuring projected scenes of moving ghosts, skeletons, and other frightening spectacles. These early projecting devices used still images linked together to mimic movement. They could not record movement from real life.

Moving Images

Photography was developed in the 1830s, but photographs could capture only a single image. Inventors tried to take a sequence of photos quickly enough to capture movement. The first person to do this successfully was Eadweard Muybridge, in 1878. He used 12 cameras in a row alongside a racetrack. As a horse ran past, its legs broke threads, triggering the cameras. This series of pictures showed the full range of the horse's gait. Muybridge also invented a machine that could project images in a rapid sequence. He mainly used painted images taken from his photographs and used the machine to illustrate his lectures. Muybridge inspired other scientists and inventors.

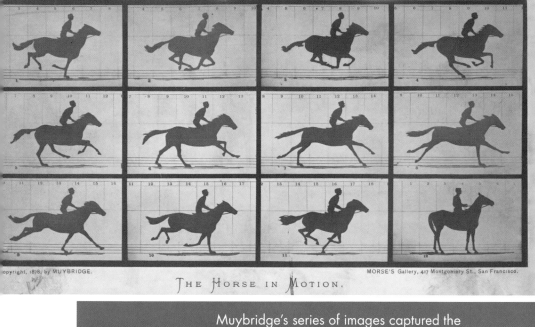

THE HORSE IN MOTION.

copyright, 1878, by MUYBRIDGE. MORSE'S Gallery, 417 Montgomery St., San Francisco.

Muybridge's series of images captured the running motion of a horse.

In the 1880s, several people made important advances in motion photography. Film on a roll replaced the glass plates formerly used in photography. A French scientist, Étienne-Jules Marey, built a mechanism to move the roll of film through a camera. In 1882, he also developed a technique to capture 12 images per second using a single camera. These images all appeared in one photograph.

Thomas Edison was already famous for many inventions, including the phonograph, used to record sound. Edison and Muybridge met in 1888 to discuss combining Muybridge's projecting machine with Edison's phonograph. Edison's original idea was to have tiny images recorded on a cylinder the size of his phonograph records. These would move on a spiral while a person watched through a microscope and listened to sound from a phonograph. Edison's staff encountered many difficulties with this method.

Then Edison met Marey and learned about his use of a flexible filmstrip. Edison and an employee, W. K. Dickson, adapted this camera into a viewer, which they called a Kinetoscope. This machine was still designed for a single user. In 1891, Edison invited people to view an image through the machine. To people who had never seen anything like it, the sight was remarkable. A viewer reported seeing "the picture of a man. . . . It bowed and smiled and waved its hands and took off its hat with the most perfect naturalness and grace. Every motion was perfect."[1]

The first Kinetoscope parlors opened in New York City in 1894. Kinetoscopes were also found in trains and bars. Customers paid from five to twenty-five cents to view short films by looking through an eyepiece into a cabinet. These films included comic sketches, historical reconstructions, and music hall sequences. Boxing matches were the most popular footage.

The Big Screen

Edison's company focused on building machines for individual viewers. It was not easy to project a movie onto a large screen so multiple people could watch it at once. The film often ripped, images blurred, and the projectors were distractingly loud.

Brothers Auguste and Louis Lumière in France showed projected motion pictures to a group audience in 1895. The program, which played ten films and lasted approximately 20 minutes, was a huge hit. Inventors in Germany, England, and the United States quickly developed cameras and projectors that could show a movie to a large group. The Kinetoscope, which could be seen by only one person at a time, began fading as a popular trend.

In 1896, Edison bought the rights to a successful machine from one of its inventors, Thomas Armat. He released it as the Vitascope, and it became the first commercially successful projector in the United

IMPRESSIONS

The Edison Vitascope premiered at Koster and Bial's Music Hall in New York City. The *New York Daily News* reported, "On the stage, when it was ready to show the invention a big drop curtain was lowered. It had a huge picture frame painted in the center with its enclosed space white. The band struck up a lively air and from overhead could be heard a whirring noise that lasted for a few moments; then there flashed upon the screen the life-size figures of two dancing girls, who tripped and pirouetted and whirled an umbrella before them. . . . The most trifling movements could be followed as accurately as if the dancers had been stepping before the audience in proper person. Even the waving undulations of their hair were plainly distinguishable."[2]

States. With the new technology, the popularity of movies grew dramatically. New York City became the center of innovation, and theaters sprang up across the United States and Europe. In response, several new projection machines were invented.

Though early audiences were impressed, films fell short of real life in several ways. Filmmakers did not yet have the ability to record sound simultaneously and play it back in sync with the images. Therefore films were silent, although typically shown with live music, lectures, or sound effects. Movies were also in black-and-white, with the exception of a very few films where every frame was painted by hand.

Most films still lasted no more than a minute. An evening's entertainment had to include other elements. Short films were shown along with live shows and magic lantern projections. They were played during lectures or at carnivals. A single film could be reproduced and shown in many places at once. Before the end of the century, films were being shown in India, Russia, China, Egypt, and Australia. The cinema became a means of global communication. Movies shared news and showed how people lived in different parts of the world.

Telling Stories

Technology was doing its part for a new industry, but for cinema to remain entertaining, it had to do more than show movement. Once the novelty of moving pictures had passed, filmmakers began experimenting with different techniques to keep audiences interested. Cinema before 1900 mostly imitated previous forms of entertainment. Many scenes were shot as if they

The Challenges of Color

Movie film originally came only in black-and-white. By 1900, a French company had developed a system to hand color film frames using stencils. Other companies tinted film in one color to give certain scenes a particular artistic feel.

The illusion of full color can be created by taking three shots of the same image, each with a different color filter: red, green, and blue. A few companies developed films that could record red and green alternating frames, but adding the third blue frame was harder. Early color films also required special projectors. Because of the poor color quality and the special equipment needed, these did not catch on.

were performed on a stage. Other films replayed events such as parades, world's fairs, and vaudeville acts. Films depicting everyday events declined in popularity as they became more common, and therefore no longer new. Filmmakers began developing new techniques and styles.

French magician Georges Méliès was responsible for several filmmaking innovations. He created the first film with more than one scene. He used dissolves and time-lapse photography. He lit scenes from the side and from above. He would sometimes layer several images to create bizarre visions, such as a gigantic hand reaching out of a cave after a running person. He was also one of the first filmmakers to write skits for actors. He added illusions to film, stopping the camera to make objects appear or disappear suddenly on screen. In one of his films, *The Vanishing Lady*, he paused the camera to substitute a skeleton for a woman.

Some early movie company owners objected to close-up film shots, feeling that customers would want to see the whole person.

Méliès is considered the originator of film genres including science fiction, horror, and comedy. In his most famous piece, *Le Voyage dans la lune*

Méliès's fantastical film tricks, as seen in movies including *Le Voyage dans la lune,* inspired many filmmakers to follow in his footsteps.

(*A Trip to the Moon,* 1902), he used original visual tricks to combine fantasy, humor, and social criticism in 30 scenes.

Only a few years after its invention, film had transitioned from a novelty that recorded life to a medium for telling increasingly complex stories. More complex storytelling, humor, and special effects slowly worked their way into short films.

The First Big Hit

Another important early filmmaker, Edwin S. Porter, started as a projectionist. By watching Méliès's *Le Voyage dans la lune*, Porter realized a film could tell a story by continuing from one scene to the next. He worked at Edison's company as a cameraman and later became director of production. Porter made films with continuous action. He often cut back and forth between simultaneous events taking place in separate locations.

Porter's film *The Great Train Robbery* (1903) introduced the Western genre and the idea of a film that told a complete story. It showed a robbery, a chase scene, and the capture of the robbers. Previously, most filmmakers recorded each scene in a single shot. Porter used multiple shots of the same scenes and edited them together using creative camera angles. The camera moved

OWNERS BEWARE

Copyright law is designed to protect intellectual property. The first motion picture copyright law was passed in 1912. Before that, it was not illegal to use another person's idea. Edison made very close copies of Méliès's films, including *Vanishing Lady*, in 1898. It was even legal to buy a print of one film and put someone else's name on it.

Photographs could be copyrighted, and some filmmakers submitted prints of film on paper rolls to the US Library of Congress. They hoped to get protection for their work under laws protecting photographs. Some early movies survive today because those prints lasted long after the filmstrips decayed.

with the action, as characters ran at and fought around it. This helped place the audience in the middle of the action. The fast pace, crime, and violence appealed to multitudes of filmgoers.

Inspired by Porter's success, filmmakers developed new ways to tell stories through moving images. This helped establish film as a primarily narrative medium. Filmmakers experimented with different camera techniques, including close-ups, point-of-view shots, and moving camera shots. Crime and chase films became popular, along with comedies and Westerns. Over the next few years, large numbers of theaters opened across the country. Cinema was here to stay.

Talking Terms

Movies, films, motion pictures, cinema—all these terms can mean essentially the same thing. A series of pictures is projected on a screen in quick succession to create the effect of a single image in which the objects move. The first known use of the term *motion picture* was in 1891. *Cinematograph* was used by 1896 to refer to the motion picture camera, projector, theater, or show. The shortened version, *cinema*, was used by 1909. It can refer to the film industry, the art of moviemaking, or the movie theater itself. The term *movie* is a shortened version of *moving picture*, and both terms were in use by 1911. The term *film* originally referred to the material that was used for taking photographs. It was later used as a verb to mean making a movie. The business of making movies may also be referred to as the film industry. This term is still used, although digital cameras no longer use film.

Chapter 3

The Birth of Hollywood

$\mathcal{O}$nce movies such as *The Great Train Robbery* proved cinema was a viable industry, both filmmakers and theater owners sought the best ways to make money. Some entrepreneurs added movies alongside slot machines and games in arcades. At the price of a nickel, the movies proved popular and made more money than the penny games. Soon business owners converted empty stores into the first movie theaters, which were called nickelodeons.

By 1908, the United States had more than 5,000 nickelodeons, many in working-class neighborhoods.[1] The greater New York area had more than 600, with an estimated 300,000 to 400,000 daily admissions.[2]

The Great Train Robbery got the film industry going with a bang.

Theater owners avoided wealthy neighborhoods and small towns, where churches and town leaders might protest this somewhat disreputable form of entertainment. Their target audience was the working class, to whom they appealed with garish posters and blaring music.

Film quality was still poor. Early projectors made the screen image flicker. The cameras were operated by hand, so the rate of movement was inconsistent. People on screen moved faster or slower than in real life. This was sometimes done deliberately for a comic effect, as was running films backward.

Feature Films

In the early days of cinema, film was wound on a reel, a cylinder that fed the film through the projector. A reel held approximately 1,000 feet (300 m) of film, enough for ten minutes.[3] Films lasted one or two reels, long enough for a quick stop during lunch or on the way home from work. Producers thought audiences would not be able to appreciate longer movies.

A 1917 nickelodeon theater entices passersby with banners and posters.

An Australian film from 1906, *The Story of the Kelly Gang*, is usually considered the first feature-length film, running 80 minutes. These more complex stories, often adaptations of literature, helped make movies respectable entertainment for the middle class. Film also began gaining recognition as an art form. Studios started producing longer films, which allowed them to develop more complex narrative techniques.

Because movies did not yet have sound, more complex stories could confuse audiences. Many cinemas used a lecturer who explained what was happening.

Some theaters had actors hidden behind the screen who yelled out dialogue and sound effects. Audiences' experiences of the same film could differ greatly from theater to theater.

Studios took back control of the story with intertitles, frames of written text. These could provide dialogue, summarize the coming action, identify a change of location, or add moral commentary, as in "Such are the wages of sin."[4] Intertitles became common by 1910 as stories became more complex.

The Studio System

In the first years of the industry, making a film was a one-person job. Most filmmakers were freelance cameramen who wrote, cast, directed,

Early Animation

In animated films, individual illustrations are photographed frame by frame. Each frame differs slightly from the preceding one. When the frames are projected in quick succession, it gives the illusion of movement. The earliest animation used hand-drawn images. The first public showing of animated cartoon films happened in Paris in 1892.

German filmmaker Lotte Reiniger animated short films for children, advertisements, and several features. She used silhouettes cut out of paper, much like shadow puppets. Her movie *The Adventures of Prince Achmed* was released in 1926. It used silhouettes instead of cartoons. It is generally considered the first feature-length animated film.

photographed, and edited their own movies.

With feature-length films, one person could no longer produce either the volume or the quality of films audiences were now demanding. Production companies were set up with a division of labor. Story departments prepared scenarios, the term used to refer to story ideas, outlines, and scripts. Some people specialized in

DIVISION OF LABOR

Léon Gaumont formed a company in France that became a model for the movie studio system. The studio's projects were created by hired writers and cinematographers and supervised by studio executives. In 1897, Gaumont's secretary, Alice Guy-Blaché, became the first female director and the first woman to head a studio production arm.

cinematography, the camera work. Other technicians took on postproduction tasks, which could include editing and adding special effects. Directors worked with the actors and camera operators, and they could bring their own artistic vision to the story. After a few years, supervisors were added to ensure the process stayed on schedule and on budget. At first supervisors were mainly former directors. Later this position got the title of producer and drew people more from business and management backgrounds. Film was an art, but film companies felt they had to control the artists involved in a film to make it a successful business.

Moviemaking quickly became an elaborate business. Hollywood sets were reproducing entire city streets by the early 1920s.

By 1914, hundreds of new companies had entered the film business. Many entrepreneurs moved west. They founded a city of filmmaking in Hollywood, a suburb outside of Los Angeles, California. Southern California offered cheap land and labor, a good climate for outdoor filming year-round, and easy access to a wide variety of scenery. Companies still famous today, including Paramount, Warner Bros., Universal, MGM, Fox, and Keystone, started there.

The World at War

Prior to World War I, many films were made in Europe, especially in France. World War I interrupted the European film industry. Some companies went out of business, while others went to work for their governments. Movie cameras were used for military reconnaissance and to produce propaganda. The war lasted from 1914 to 1918 in Europe, resulting in a major loss of personnel, resources, and markets. By the end of the war, as Europe struggled to rebuild, Hollywood emerged as the center of moviemaking. Many Europeans in the industry, from actors to directors to lighting technicians, moved to California after the war.

INTERNATIONAL IDEAS

While Hollywood was growing as a center of moviemaking in the first decades of the 1900s, other countries also had strong film industries and innovative approaches. Germany introduced Expressionism on screen. This art movement tried to capture internal states of mind by depicting dark hallucinations. Russian filmmakers used editing in new ways. Clashing images could express ideas and provoke intellectual and emotional reactions.

The Star System

Originally, movies did not list the actors' names, perhaps out of fear that popular actors would ask for higher salaries. But audiences began attending movies to see their favorite actors. Studios recognized that stars brought in audiences, and therefore earned more money for the movies. Star salaries rose. Comic actor Charlie Chaplin went from making $130 a week in 1913 to $10,000 a week in 1914.[5]

People became intensely interested in the lives of stars, and studios manipulated stories for the press. Studios even attempted to manufacture stars. Theodosia Goodman, the daughter of a Cincinnati tailor, was transformed into Theda Bara, supposedly the child of a French artist and an Arab woman.

Some of these early stars were active in other aspects of the movie business as well. Mary Pickford started in live theater as a teenager. She quickly adapted to the different needs of the movie screen. She toned down the exaggerated gestures of the theater and expressed emotion through her eyes instead. She rose to fame on the screen with her beauty, glamour, girlish sweetness, and feisty determination. Fan magazines helped feed the public's fascination with cinema's first celebrity. A journalist described her as "the woman who was known

Charlie Chaplin, *seated*, with D. W. Griffith, Mary Pickford, and Douglas Fairbanks, *front row standing, left to right*, sign the contract establishing United Artists.

to more people and loved by more people than any other woman that has been in all history."[6]

Pickford married popular actor Douglas Fairbanks in 1920, and they became known as the king and queen of Hollywood. Together with Charlie Chaplin and director D. W. Griffith, they established United Artists. The company distributed films by its founders, bringing more control and profit to the performers.

The Birth
of a Nation

D. W. Griffith adapted a novel by Thomas Dixon, *The Clansman*, into the film *The Birth of a Nation*. Griffith developed the technique of crosscutting between two different lines of action. This added drama, as in scenes that cut between people in trouble and their rescuers rushing to save them. Griffith also used close-ups of actors' faces to capture emotion; battle scenes shot on location; and soft lighting and backlighting for effect.

The Birth of a Nation was also socially controversial. The movie told the story of two white families divided by the Civil War. Slavery was portrayed positively, and belonging to the white supremacist group the Ku Klux Klan was depicted as honorable. The movie led to protests and even riots in some cities when it was shown.

The film ran more than three hours, cost $100,000 to make, and earned $18 million.[7] Despite the controversy, the movie showed films could be popular, profitable, and powerful.

The controversially racist film *The Birth of a Nation* was also a showcase of technical and artistic innovation.

By the 1920s, Hollywood was the film capital of the world. America produced more than 800 films on average each year.[8] Nearly all films shown in the United States were produced in Hollywood. By the end of the decade, 80 million Americans were going to the movies every week, a huge number that was approximately 65 percent of the US population at the time.[9] Movie stars were famous worldwide, and Hollywood became synonymous with the movie industry.

African-American Films

Largely ignored by early Hollywood or portrayed in racist terms, African Americans instead developed their own film culture. Their movies used the same genres as Hollywood but were by and for black people. These films generally had low budgets and were played in black neighborhood theaters in cities such as Detroit, Michigan, and Chicago, Illinois.

Oscar Micheaux, the most famous African-American filmmaker of the time, wrote, produced, and directed more than 45 films. He made *The Homesteader* (1919), a film version of his novel about farming. This was the first full-length feature produced by an African American. His second film, *Within Our Gates* (1920), was a response to *Birth of a Nation*. Micheaux's film shows that in reality, whites at the time were more likely to harm blacks than the other way around.

Chapter 4

The Golden Age of Talkies

The advent of sound technology at the end of the 1920s hugely transformed the film industry. According to film historian Robert Sklar, "No single innovation has come close to being regarded as a similar kind of watershed."[1] Yet at the time, some critics believed sound film was a novelty that would quickly fade.

Previous attempts to add recorded sound had failed because of technical problems. The 1920s saw many advances in electronics and telecommunications. Sound-on-film provided the necessary breakthrough. It involved turning sound waves into images. The movie projector could read those images and convert them back into sounds. Because the sound was recorded right

Singer Al Jolson starred in the first talkie, or full-length movie with sound, in 1927.

alongside the images, they were automatically in sync. Improvements followed quickly.

The First Talkie

Sound was first used in short films, which provided an opportunity to work out technical challenges. The first feature-length movie with synchronized sound was released in 1927. *The Jazz Singer* opened with actor Al Jolson singing and then saying, "Wait a minute. Wait a minute. You ain't heard nothing yet."[2] The film had only two scenes of dialogue, plus Jolson singing and playing the piano. Intertitles were still used for dialogue in other scenes. The story appealed to audiences

Speaking Up

Some stars of the silent era transitioned well to talkies. Others struggled. The ability to portray soulful emotions purely through expression was no longer so important. Personality came through in dialogue. Many new actors came from live theater.

Studios required beginning actors to sign contracts to only work with an individual studio. These contracts paid better than the theater, and much better than average wages.

However, the new stars made much less than stars of the 1920s. Actors on contract with a studio did not get to choose which roles they played. Studios manipulated their public personas as well. Publicity staffs sent photos and articles to newspapers and magazines. They fed juicy items to gossip columnists. Fans wanted drama, so performers could not count on only good news being released.

regardless. Jolson played a
young Jewish man who wants
to sing jazz music rather than
follow the family tradition
of singing in the synagogue.
He also falls in love with
a woman of a different
religion. The movie addressed

conflicts between immigrant parents and US-born
children. Jolson's character struggles to reconcile his
Jewish and American identities. The movie pitted new
popular culture against traditional arts. It also proved
talking films were more than a fad.

Making sound movies was a challenge at first.
Noisy cameras had to be soundproofed, which reduced
the director's ability to move the camera. Actors had
to stand an appropriate distance from a microphone
hidden on the set. Early sound films might have distant
shots of actors moving without speaking, followed by
shots where they stood still and spoke. Still, audiences
demanded more movies with sound, which soon became
known as talkies. The technical problems were quickly
overcome. Microphones were hung from long moveable
arms that dangled above the scene. Cameras went on

battery-operated dollies with rubber tires. Later, quieter cameras were developed. Soon movies could have both sound and action.

One side effect of adding sound to movies was that films could no longer be understood in every language. In Europe, films were often dubbed. New dialogue was recorded over the film, using the local language. In the United States, foreign films more often had translations printed across the bottom of the screen.

Beautiful Technicolor

The 1920s saw the beginnings of other innovations, though none of these were firmly established until decades later. New color processes were explored. All colors can be made from a combination of red, green, and blue. Technicolor used a combination of red and green images recorded simultaneously. The inventors could not at first figure out how to add a third color, so the color appeared washed-out. Still, Technicolor became the primary color technology. The first feature-length film completely in Technicolor came out in 1922. In 1930, approximately 30 films came out with part or all color.[4] Many companies worked on improving color film through the following years. Various systems were cumbersome or expensive, until Kodak's easier-to-use Eastman film debuted in 1948.

Early Technicolor cameras did not use color film. They filmed in black-and-white, with two different colored filters and two filmstrips. The light entered the camera lens, and a mirror split the beam in two. Half went through a red filter and half went through a blue-green filter. The filters took out some of the colors from the light. Through this process, each filter tinted its own filmstrip. The filmstrips were then processed with color dye. Finally, the two filmstrips were glued together, and the combination provided a color image.

Later Technicolor added a third filter. A special camera ran three separate strips of film at the same time. This provided more realistic color.

Genres Still Rule

As film culture progressed in the 1920s, Hollywood movie production focused on the concept of genre. The first question asked when planning a film was, "What kind of film is it?" Genres included comedy, drama, mystery, love story, and Western. Genres broke down into subgenres, so a comedy could be slapstick, parody, farce, or sophisticated. These categories came from novels, magazine stories, and the theater. Each genre had a characteristic subject, style, or technique. Genres could be combined, as in comedy drama or romantic drama. Audiences knew what to expect, and they

Actor and director Buster Keaton was famous for his 1920s comedies.

enjoyed stories that stayed within genre limits, although they expected some fresh variations.

Over the course of movie history, genres have risen and fallen in popularity. They might reflect historical or cultural influences. For example, Westerns, science fiction, and horror have all flourished in various periods. In some cases, one successful movie may set off a trend of imitators in that genre.

After World War I, cartoons were often played before feature films. The first big animation star was Felix the Cat, created in 1919 by Otto Messmer. Artist Walt Disney produced many animated cartoons in the 1920s. Walt, his brother Roy, and cartoonist Ub Iwerks started the Disney Brothers' Studio and created Mickey Mouse. They produced two cartoons in 1928 but could not find a distributor. Then they made the Mickey Mouse cartoon *Steamboat Willie* later the same year. This was the first animated cartoon with synchronized sound. In one scene, a goat swallowed sheet music. Minnie Mouse cranked its tail to release the sound. Mickey was on his way to worldwide fame.

Walt Disney and Snow White

Walt Disney's film *Snow White and the Seven Dwarfs*, released in 1937, was noteworthy in several areas. It was the first full-length animated feature in color and with sound. It was technically brilliant and innovative. A multiplane camera allowed several layers of artwork to move past the camera at different speeds. This created the illusion of depth. Human characters were modeled on live actors. The film took nearly four years to produce, at a cost of $1.7 million, making it outrageously expensive for the time. During production, it was called "Disney's Folly." However, the movie was commercially successful and the innovation earned Walt Disney an honorary Academy Award in 1939. It was the first film to release a motion picture soundtrack album. When the movie was released on home video in 1994, it became the best-selling videocassette of all time, with 50 million copies sold worldwide.[5]

Snow White and the Seven Dwarfs has enchanted generations of audiences.

Shocking Sensibilities

The 1930s began with a terrible economic depression and ended with a world at war. Still, movie attendance and profits went up in 1930 over the previous year. The talkies were new and thrilling enough to bring in audiences. Profits dropped for the next two years, however. Ticket prices were lowered from thirty cents to twenty cents on average. By 1933, nearly a third of all theaters had closed.

Studios attempted to draw in larger audiences with more shocking and risqué films. Sound could provide sensational and emotional effects. Crime films reverberated with shattering glass, screeching tires, sirens, gunfire, and screams. Dialogue included sexual references and jokes. Scantily clad chorus girls appeared in musicals.

A backlash followed against depictions of behavior deemed immoral. Censorship had always been an issue in the movie business. In the early 1930s, Roman Catholic

The most profitable films of the 1930s starred children and teenagers, such as Shirley Temple, Deanna Durbin, and Mickey Rooney.

clergymen took over the fight for morality. They set up a nationwide organization called the Legion of Decency. In 1934, millions of people signed forms pledging to boycott movies the group considered indecent. Studios, already hurt by the depression, gave in. They agreed to self-regulate, following a strict code of morals. The code allowed crimes such as adultery and murder, but the crimes could not be portrayed in a sympathetic way, and the guilty had to be punished. This allowed studios to keep producing films with the crime and sex that brought in audiences while also following middle-class moral standards.

The code addressed many other behaviors. Interracial romance, homosexuality, abortion, and drugs were prohibited. Profanity was restricted, along with many words defined as vulgar,

Anti-Semitism

Hollywood has often reflected American attitudes, including racism and discrimination. Jewish immigrants were active in the movie business from its earliest days, and many studio heads were Jewish immigrants. Several waves of hatred have targeted Jews in the film industry. In the 1920s, many movies reflected the Jazz Age, with its more permissive morality. Some people felt these movies were corrupting American youth. People with this attitude blamed this on the Jewish heads of some of the major studios. In reality, the producers and stars most associated with scandal were typically not Jewish.

including *sex*. These restrictions prevented filmmakers from portraying many real issues. Instead, Hollywood created a glamorous, idealized world on screen.

America Escapes

Times were hard in the United States during the Great Depression. Politicians called on Hollywood to accentuate the positive. The mayor of New York asked movie exhibitors to "show pictures which will reinstate courage and hope in the hearts of the people."[6] Studios had more practical concerns. They knew they could appeal to bigger audiences, and therefore earn more money, by offering an escape from stress.

The screwball comedy saw new life. These films could include satire and sexuality, but in the end they promoted traditional gender roles and social order. Heroines discovered marriage was better than a career. Rich characters were harmless and lovable. These movies showed it was all right to have fun, but you shouldn't take things too far. Many comedy classics still popular today were released between 1934 and 1940. These include *My Man Godfrey*, *Bringing Up Baby*, *Holiday*, and *His Girl Friday*. They made stars of Cary

KATHARINE **HEPBURN**
CARY **GRANT**
in a **HOWARD HAWKS**
production of
BRINGING UP BABY
with
Charlie **RUGGLES** · *Barry* **FITZGERALD** · *May* **ROBSON** · *Walter* **CATLETT**

The comedy *Bringing Up Baby* stars Katharine Hepburn, Cary Grant, and a pet leopard named Baby.

Grant, Carole Lombard, and Katharine Hepburn, among others.

Another trend featured dignified historical dramas and adaptations from literature. Films adapted books such as *Anna Karenina*, *David Copperfield*, *Mutiny on the Bounty*, *Gone with the Wind*, and *A Tale of Two Cities*. Studio head David O. Selznick claimed, "There are only two kinds of merchandise that can be made profitably in this business—either the very cheap pictures or the expensive pictures."[7] Although there were exceptions, that concept had merit. A big-budget picture, with famous stars, elaborate costumes and sets, and strong marketing, would probably make money. Popular novels and famous events from history worked well as big productions. Cheap movies might also make more than they cost, but films with medium-sized budgets often did not attract enough of an audience to turn a profit. To some extent, this division remains in the movie industry today.

Critics today debate whether movies were actually better during this so-called Golden Age of Hollywood. Quality aside, movies presented an image of glamour. Americans embraced the image, and so did people around the world. The influence of American movies as a cultural phenomenon cannot be underestimated. According to film historian Robert Sklar, American movies after World War I had a voice beyond any other means of communication. "No military power, no imperial administration, had cast its leadership so far and wide. Only the world's great religions had comparable reach."[8] The best films of the era are still popular today.

Chapter 5

Struggle to Survive

Technology and attitudes continued changing rapidly in the middle of the 1900s. The Great Depression gave way to World War II (1939–1945), which had both positive and negative effects on the movie industry. The United States entered the war in December 1941. By this point, film was a popular medium, and world governments recognized its power. Propaganda had the most effect when disguised as entertainment. Many countries promoted political views through wartime films. Newsreels and documentaries showed wartime activity. Combat was filmed for military analysis.

Many Hollywood filmmakers worked on documentaries for the military and government.

Pop culture contributed to the war effort during World War II,
even including cartoons such as Bugs Bunny.

Humphrey Bogart and Ingrid Bergman star in *Casablanca*.

One series, *Why We Fight*, explained the factors that led to the war and promoted the goals of the United States. This series, directed by Frank Capra, was shown to all US Army soldiers and was also released publicly.

Even popular movies supported the war effort. In the United States, the new Office of War Information worked with Hollywood studios to promote political goals. These included persuading Americans that the war was a just cause and deserved their support. Some films showed diverse groups working together to win the war. Others portrayed the bravery and patience of those waiting at home while loved ones fought. Even cartoon figures supported the war effort. Bugs Bunny, a creation of Warner Bros. studio, tackled the enemy in several cartoons.

Perhaps the most famous and popular World War II movie is *Casablanca* (1942). The movie's events start shortly before the 1941 Japanese attack on Pearl Harbor that spurred US involvement in the war. Rick, played by Humphrey Bogart, is an American running a nightclub in Casablanca, Morocco. The film shows his change from cynical and bitter to a heroic patriot.

Hollywood studios made nearly as many feature films during the war years as previously. An average of 440 features were released each year from 1942

Preserving Classic Films

Motion picture film decays over time. Many important and famous early movies have deteriorated over the years. Early studios often did not even try to preserve many films. Reels were thrown away or shuffled into storage. Some films have no remaining copies, or the only copies are so worn they cannot be duplicated. By some estimates, 50 percent of the films made before 1950 have been lost.[1] Early color film faded quickly, so many of those movies have since been damaged or lost.

Film preservationists work to save these films. This is a complex and difficult process, and it is not happening fast enough to save every classic film. Modern digital media should help preserve current movies for the future, though digital formats change quickly.

to 1944.[2] Movie theater attendance rose during the war. Employment was up due to new jobs supporting the war effort. With many resources rationed, people did not have many options for spending their money. Movies were a popular form of entertainment. In some places, theaters were open around the clock to serve factory workers getting off late-night shifts.

After the War

After the war, some filmmakers broke away from the big Hollywood studios. Prominent director Frank Capra was one of many who saw too little variety in Hollywood. He claimed independent production would bring new quality and innovation. Other directors and actors, including Humphrey Bogart, set up their own companies. However, many of these small companies struggled. When success depended on a single film, delays or budget overruns were disastrous. Without large financial backing, one mistake could prove fatal for a company.

The political climate was changing in ways that would challenge Hollywood. The US had allied with the Soviet Union, a Communist country, during World War II. After the war, tension arose and the two countries entered what is called a cold war. While not officially at war, the United States and the Soviet Union were engaged in a political and military rivalry. During the Cold War, many people believed communism was a serious threat to US security.

The US House of Representatives implemented the House Un-American Activities Committee (HUAC). The HUAC investigated the American Communist Party for illegal or immoral activities. The American Communist Party had developed in 1919 and was a legal political party in the United States. However, in 1947, more than 40 members of the film industry were

Overseas Markets

Foreign markets have always been important to Hollywood studios. Before World War II, American movie studios earned up to 40 percent of their total box office revenues from outside the Untied States and Canada.³ The European market declined during the war. Studios were able to keep up their profits because of increased attendance in the United States. They also expanded into Latin America.

After the war, studios hoped to exploit the reopened European markets. In 1948, Italy imported 668 feature films from the United States.⁴ However, European countries wanted to support their own national film businesses. The United Kingdom, France, and Italy restricted foreign film imports. This limited the overseas market for Hollywood. In some countries, American studios were allowed to make more money if they then spent that money in the country. This led US studios to film more overseas.

DRIVE-INS

The drive-in theater became a popular midcentury trend. These theaters consisted of a large outdoor movie screen, a concession stand, and a parking area. Customers viewed movies from their cars. The first drive-in opened in 1934. As more Americans got cars, drive-in theaters grew from approximately 100 theaters in the United States in 1946 to 5,000 by 1956. Some offered family night for one dollar for as many people as would fit in the car.[6] Many people enjoyed the flexibility of drive-in theaters. They could bring noisy babies and young children, and cars had larger seats than regular theaters. Drive-in theaters were often built at the edges of towns. As those towns grew, land prices rose and many drive-ins went out of business. A few hundred drive-in theaters still exist in the 2000s.

called to a hearing and asked if they were members of the Communist Party.[5] Because it was not illegal to be a Communist, some members refused to answer. They argued the First Amendment protected the privacy of their political beliefs. Ten prominent directors and screenwriters, dubbed the Hollywood Ten, were charged with contempt of Congress for refusing to answer the question. All of them served up to a year in prison.

To avoid more government interference, the movie industry agreed to stop employing Communists. Further investigations added more people to the blacklist, even though many had no proven links to the Communist Party. Some banned scriptwriters continued writing under other names. Actors and producers did not have that option. Many careers were damaged. The blacklist continued until the 1960s.

Several other factors contributed to declining movie attendance after the war. The US population shifted to the suburbs, farther from theaters. War veterans focused on working and starting families and had less time and money for entertainment. With more people owning automobiles, interest grew in travel and outdoor activities. Television became more widespread starting around 1948. By 1953, nearly half of American families owned television sets. This offered an alternate form of entertainment. Movie attendance dropped to approximately half of its 1946 high point.

Technology as an Answer

The movie industry tried to find new ways to lure audiences into the theater. In 1948, Kodak released a color film. The film did not have the color range of Technicolor, but it was more easily developed and copied. More color pictures were made. Color television

The one and only Smell-O-Vision movie came out in 1960. Signals on the film triggered the scents in the theater.

3-D films captured audiences' attention for a short while in the 1950s.

was not perfected until 1953, and shows were not widely aired in color until the 1960s. It took until 1972 for sales of color televisions to exceed black-and-white sales. Until then, color movies offered something special.

All the major studios started making 3-D films in 1953. The technology and the movies were both low quality, and viewers found wearing the 3-D glasses uncomfortable. The novelty quickly wore off and the trend faded. Hollywood studios released 23 features in 3-D in 1953 but only one in 1955.[7] Studios also explored different screen formats.

Animation was becoming more popular than ever in the 1940s and 1950s. After the success of *Snow White*, Disney released *Pinocchio*, featuring a wooden puppet who wants to be a real boy, in 1940. The film won two Academy Awards, for Best Original Score and Best Song, and was the highest-earning film of the year. Later that year Disney released *Fantasia*, which had seven separate animated stories each set to their own piece of classical music. Mickey Mouse made his only appearance in a feature cartoon as the star of one segment, *The Sorcerer's Apprentice*. Disney released more feature-length animated movies in the 1940s, including *Dumbo* and *Bambi*. The 1950s brought classics such as *Cinderella*, *Lady and the Tramp*, and *Peter Pan*, which were the top three grossing films of the decade.

ANIMATION EVERYWHERE

Disney was not the only animation company. William Hanna and Joseph Barbera released more than 100 cartoons featuring Tom and Jerry between 1940 and 1958. Animator Walter Lantz introduced Woody Woodpecker in 1940. The manic, aggressive bird starred in 200 short cartoons over three decades.[8]

The Warner Bros. studio began releasing cartoons in 1930. It eventually produced the Looney Tunes and Merrie Melodies series. Famous directors included Chuck Jones and Tex Avery. Famous characters included Bugs Bunny, Daffy Duck, Porky Pig, the Tasmanian Devil, and Yosemite Sam.

GOLDEN AGE
of Genre

Musicals were popular in the 1950s, by which time films had reliable sound and color. The 1952 hit *Singin' in the Rain* looked back at the birth of the talkies. Comedies remained strong, often with light or wacky stories.

Westerns saw a revival in the 1950s and 1960s. Action-adventure movies became one of the most important formulas. The James Bond series was popular throughout the 1960s. These movies portrayed a new kind of glamour, with special effects, shooting in exotic locations, and open sexuality.

Science-fiction films were inspired by the 1950s interest in space travel and rocketry. They also reflected anxiety over the dangers of nuclear power and nuclear war. Science fiction inspired many special-effects techniques. These included miniature sets, model figures, stop-action shooting, and the blue-screen process. The most enduring science-fiction movie of the era was *Invasion of the Body Snatchers*, from 1956.

Chapter 6

Changing Morals

*I*n the 1950s, studios produced fewer movies, focusing more on formulas designed to be big hits. That meant making films in popular genres, especially those that could offer spectacular visual effects and costumes. These would look better on the big screen, so they could compete with television. Hollywood was appealing to a more educated middle class. Popular Broadway musicals and best-selling novels seemed natural for movie adaptation since they were already familiar. The American film industry praised these "prestige" pictures, and they were the type that won awards.

Big budget musicals, such as *The Sound of Music*, were common during the 1950s and 1960s.

Revising Genre

Hollywood struggled to find a formula for success. The decline in the movie business that started in the 1950s hit hard in the 1960s. By 1960, weekly movie attendance had fallen 63 percent from its peak in 1946.[1] Average attendance began stabilizing at less than half the numbers of the 1950s.[2] Before World War II, the average number of feature films produced each year had been close to 500. In 1959, the number dropped

The Oscars

The first Academy Awards ceremony was held in 1929. The awards honored different aspects of films and filmmaking. The 230 members of the Academy chose 10 nominees for each of 12 different categories. A central board of judges made the final selection of winners, who were all notified in advance of the ceremony.

That ceremony was not broadcast. The next year, the awards could be heard on a local radio station, and they were played on national radio beginning in 1933. They were broadcast on television starting in 1953. The movie industry was reluctant to share the ceremony with its rival television, but financial considerations won out. The Academy received $100,000 for the broadcast rights.[3] In addition, the telecast acted as promotion for the winning movies.

The 1953 show brought in the most viewers for any program up to that time. The format has changed over the years, but the Academy Awards remains a popular television event. Winners receive a statue, known as Oscar, which gave the award its nickname.

below 200.[4] In 1963, only 121 feature films were made in Hollywood.[5] Fewer films meant fewer jobs in the film industry and lower profits.

Despite lower movie attendance, Hollywood was still a major power in world film production. Studios continued the 1950s trend of making big-budget extravaganzas, often based on Broadway musicals. Sometimes this worked well: *The Sound of Music* (1965) made nearly twice as much as any previous movie. Yet a big budget was not a guarantee of success. *Cleopatra* (1963) was perhaps the most expensive movie in history at $44 million (worth more than $300 million today when adjusted for inflation).[6] Long but with a choppy, disorganized plot, the film lost $10 million.[7]

As the 1960s progressed, more genre films broke away from traditional genre rules. Director John Ford, who had been making Westerns since 1917, challenged American myths about the West. *Sergeant Rutledge* (1960) features a black cavalry soldier, showing the role of African Americans in western expansion. In *Cheyenne Autumn* (1964), a small group of Cheyenne try to escape a reservation and return to their home territory. *The Man Who Shot Liberty Valance* (1962) shows how legends, even false ones, can become part of history.

Contemporary films touched on racial issues as well. In 1967, two films featured African-American actor Sidney Poitier. He played a homicide detective in *In the Heat of the Night* and a scientist engaged to a white woman in *Guess Who's Coming to Dinner*. In both films, hostile white people come to recognize his worth and accept him.

Other cultural movements found a voice in film. Feminism was on the rise. Biographies, autobiographies, and historical pieces shared insight into the movement's current leaders and forgotten heroes.

News and Information

Television had become the primary source of news and information in America. While this hurt the movie theater business, television networks developed documentary films for television broadcast. This led to a renaissance of nonfiction filmmaking. Documentaries are not always factual, however. The choice

NATIVE AMERICANS ON FILM

In the first half of the 1900s, Hollywood portrayed Native Americans as the enemy. They attacked wagon trains and stagecoaches in dozens of Westerns. Starting in 1950, some films took a more sympathetic view as society became more aware of social injustice. However, even these films showed native life through a European-American perspective. Most major Native American roles were played by European Americans. *Dances with Wolves* (1991) cast more Native Americans than any previous movie. Yet it still tells their story through the experiences of a white man.

Sidney Poitier was the first black person to win an Academy Award for Best Actor.

of what to include and how to show it determines the film's viewpoint. Some films dramatize potential horrors rather than reporting the current truth. Music and voice-overs can affect the mood of a film. Documentaries are used to manipulate as well as inform.

Feature films also addressed war in a new way. *MASH* (1970) was set during the Korean War (1950–1953). It combined new attitudes about sex and violence and a cynicism about war in a dark comedy. Though it did not directly address the Vietnam War, it portrayed war in general with more cynicism than most earlier war films.

Youth Culture

Another significant movie of the era was *The Graduate*. Released in 1967, it was the second-highest-earning film of the decade. It features a 20-year-old college graduate who has an affair with an older woman. The young man, played by Dustin Hoffman, is drifting in life. He does not understand the rules of his parents' generation. The music soundtrack was provided by Simon and Garfunkel, a folk-rock band whose music addressed social and political issues.

The Graduate touched a chord in the younger generation. Its success convinced movie studios they were overlooking an important segment of the audience. In the late 1960s, several movies targeted young people with daring stories. *Easy Rider* (1969) features two drug dealers traveling America on their motorcycles to a soundtrack of popular rock songs. *Midnight Cowboy* (1969) received an X rating (no one under 16 admitted at that time) for its portrayal of prostitution, drug use, and homosexuality. The movie won three Academy Awards, for Best Picture, Best Director, and Best Adapted Screenplay. It became the only X-rated movie ever to win an Academy Award.

These movies reflected the changes in morality of the era. More open sexuality was accepted in books, advertising, and public behavior. The United States was moving away from the standards that had been promoted by the censorship code. In 1968, the code was replaced by a rating system. Under the earlier code, representatives had supervised scripts, lyrics, and costumes before a movie was made. The rating system only reviews movies after they are finished. It was conceived as an advisory system for parents, and theaters were not required to enforce the age limits.

American culture was changing. Movies both promoted the change and reflected it.

Easy Rider was one of a number of late–1960s films targeting youth in a new way.

Chapter 7

Building the Blockbuster

Movies had been changing along with American culture. But it was a business change that really made a difference in ticket sales. In the early 1970s, Hollywood studios altered their distribution methods. Previously, films were released in only a few cities at a time. Over the course of a year, a film would move from larger to smaller theaters—the rolls of film passed down the chain as larger theaters finished with them. In the 1970s, films were released widely. The same movie could be shown simultaneously in small towns and big cities. This meant it cost studios more to print many copies of the film, so studios required a higher percentage of ticket sales. That expense was worthwhile

Jaws (1975) is considered the first blockbuster.

to small theaters, since they could make popular new films available right away.

Jaws (1975), directed by Steven Spielberg, was one of the first films to be released widely. The horror film about a shark attacking vacationing swimmers was number one for 14 consecutive weeks. It became the first film to earn more than $100 million in domestic box office.[1] Its success inspired studios to make more summer blockbuster movies, when summer had previously been seen as a slow time.

New publicity methods supported this change. Studios recognized the power of television for reaching an audience. A strong television ad campaign could get people across the country talking about the same movie at once. Theater companies built multiplex theaters where several films could be shown every night. People now had choices at their local theater every week.

Talking about Movies

Film criticism has been around since the beginning of cinema. The New York Film Critics Circle was founded in 1935. But film criticism reached new heights in 1975 when Roger Ebert and Gene Siskel debuted their movie review show. *Coming Soon to a Theater Near You* lasted for 36 years in various incarnations and under different names. Part of the show's appeal came from the fact that the two men often disagreed, and they shared their passion for movies with the audience.

Choices meant competition between movies. With ticket sales still low, studios needed to attract as many viewers as possible. They focused on the growing youth market. A baby boom had followed World War II when returning veterans started families, meaning by the 1960s there was a large and still growing contingent of US teenagers.

To attract this audience, studios started recruiting young directors, many of whom had recently graduated from film schools. These young filmmakers were schooled in traditional cinema standards and methods, but they also felt free to push boundaries. Some movies were dark and pessimistic, with moral ambiguity. Many explored issues of power, both personal and institutional. Important movies included *The Godfather* and *The Godfather Part II*, *Chinatown*, *One Flew over the Cuckoo's Nest*, *Taxi Driver*, and *All the President's Men*. Some film critics have suggested the 1970s were a second "Golden Age" for Hollywood. Directors George Lucas, Francis Ford Coppola, Steven Spielberg, and Martin Scorsese got their start in that era. They all found success by age 30 and went on to have long careers.

As movies more often targeted youth, films started breaking records for ticket sales. Young people would

Steven Spielberg, *left*, and George Lucas were two up-and-coming directors in the 1970s.

return to see a film multiple times. Tie-in products such as toys and clothing added yet more revenue. Films came out based on popular comic books, such as *Superman* (1978). Sequels had existed before, but they came out in greater numbers to take advantage of name recognition. Special effects also attracted a younger crowd.

Star Wars (1977) captivated audiences and blasted away box office records. Most previous blockbusters featured big stars and had been based on well-known sources, such as Broadway musicals or novels. *Star Wars* was written by its director, George Lucas, and its actors were largely unknown. Science fiction was not usually a leading genre. But the movie had special effects that were astonishing for the time, incorporated into a feel-good story that countered the prevailing dark cynicism of the 1970s.

Lucas as producer teamed with Spielberg as director for another adventure series. *Raiders of the Lost Ark* (1981) and its sequels had a historical setting, but they also depended on fantasy elements and special effects. Spielberg then made *E.T. the Extra-Terrestrial* (1982), which brought the same elements to the story of an alien lost in the California suburbs. It was the most successful film in history then and for the next 15 years.

Lucas and Spielberg could be called the directing stars of the 1970s and 1980s. By the end of the 1980s, the two had been involved with eight of the top ten box office hits of all time. Spielberg directed five of them, while Lucas directed one and produced five others.[2]

Film budgets rose dramatically in the 1980s, in the hope that more money spent would mean more success. However, of movies that cost $14 million or more to produce, only a quarter earned back their production costs at the US box office.[3]

GEORGE LUCAS'S
Galaxy

Harrison Ford, Carrie Fisher, and Mark Hamill, *left to right*, in *Star Wars*, 1977

George Lucas studied cinematography at the University of Southern California. There he produced a short science-fiction film. Director and producer Francis Ford Coppola persuaded Warner Bros. to make a full-length version of the film. *THX-1138* (1971) was a flop, but Lucas went on to have success with *American Graffiti* (1973).

Lucas wanted to make a fantasy adventure set in outer space. The project started as an idea for a children's Saturday morning series and evolved into a full-length feature film. When *Star Wars* was released in 1977, audiences were enthralled by the characters, landscapes, and special effects. The film, made for $11 million, grossed more than $500 million worldwide during its original release.[4] The story continued in *The Empire Strikes Back* (1980) and *The Return of the Jedi* (1983), three prequels in the 1990s and 2000s, and several new films planned for the 2010s.

Some films found more success over time. *Blade Runner* (1982), by British director Ridley Scott, was not very successful at first. But the futuristic film noir later became a cult classic, admired by both fans and critics.

Reasons to Stay Home

Technology has always played an important part in the history of cinema. At first it brought people into theaters. Later, it allowed them to stay home.

Although television became widespread in the 1950s, it mainly reached people in larger cities. Small towns and rural locations got poor reception. Cable television began as a way to transmit network television to those areas. In the 1970s, cable networks began providing new television programs. This provided viewers with more choices than the original three broadcast networks, ABC, CBS, and NBC. By 1990, there were 79 networks, and 57 percent of households with televisions subscribed to cable. By 2012, there were 800 networks.[5]

The Walt Disney Company earned more from video sales of *Beauty and the Beast* (1991) than any film had ever earned from movie ticket sales at that time.

Some networks play movies that were first released in theaters. Popular movies might play on television for years, and films that struggled in the theater have a second chance. Movies no longer have to make money only in theaters.

Other technical revolutions had lasting effects on the film industry. In 1977, the Video Home System (VHS) was introduced in North America. Videocassette recorders could be used to play home movies or to watch films taped from television broadcasts. By 1992, 76 percent of homes had videocassette recorders.[6]

Video stores sprang up across the country to rent or sell movies on video. At first Hollywood saw the VHS as a threat to movie attendance. Then studios recognized the potential for making money from video sales. Some films sold millions of copies to individuals with home movie libraries. Earnings could be higher from video sales than from theater showings. In 1986, the film industry began making more money from video sales than from movie tickets. In 1992, Americans spent $12 billion to buy or rent videotapes. This was two and a half times the $4.9 billion spent on box office ticket sales.[7]

The world market also became more important for American films. Some films that did poorly in the

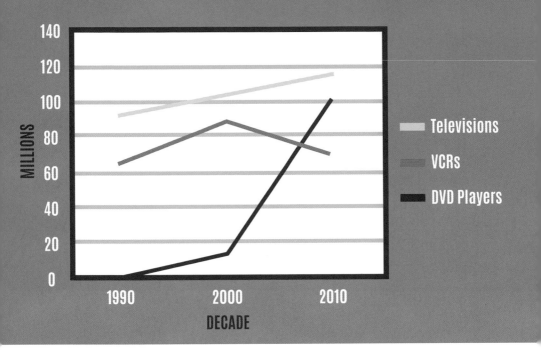

Televisions, VCRs, and DVD Players in US Homes[8]

MILLIONS

▬▬	Televisions
▬▬	VCRs
▬▬	DVD Players

DECADE

United States and Canada did better in the rest of the world. A US box-office flop might turn into a hit when foreign ticket sales, video sales, and cable television revenue were added up.

The World on Film

All these technological changes helped bring a wider variety of movies to more people. In the early part of the 1900s, Americans saw foreign countries primarily through the lens of white, male, American filmmakers. As the century drew to a close, world cinema was finding a home in the United States. Films from many countries saw box office success, no longer only playing at colleges and art-house theaters. Europe was not the only continent to share successful films with the world, either. Movies from Latin America, Asia, and Africa played on television and were sold on video. Voices from around the world were speaking for themselves.

And Americans were listening. The 1998 film *Life Is Beautiful* is an improbable comedy about the Holocaust by Italian director Roberto Benigni. It broke earnings records for foreign-language films in the United States. Then the martial arts film *Crouching Tiger, Hidden Dragon*, by Taiwanese director Ang Lee, came out in 2000. The film broke US genre conventions by showing strong female warriors and appealing to an audience that would not normally view martial arts films. It became the most successful foreign-language film of all time at the US box office, earning $60 million in the United States. It was also nominated for ten Oscars and won four.[9]

ANIME

Anime, a style of Japanese animation, became popular in America starting in the 1980s. These films often combine rich characters with magical or mystical settings. Animator Hayao Miyazaki is known as the Japanese Walt Disney. His *Spirited Away* (2001) was the first anime feature film to win an Academy Award.

Chapter 8

Independent Films

*W*hile blockbusters dominated Hollywood, smaller films followed their own trajectory. Independent production companies have a long history in Hollywood. These smaller companies focus on lower budget, more artistic films than those produced by the big studios. The French term *avant-garde* is sometimes applied to films that are more concerned with experimenting with film form than they are with telling a clear story. During World War II, many European avant-garde filmmakers moved to the United States. An "underground" film culture developed in the following years. Communities sprang up to make, watch, and discuss films made

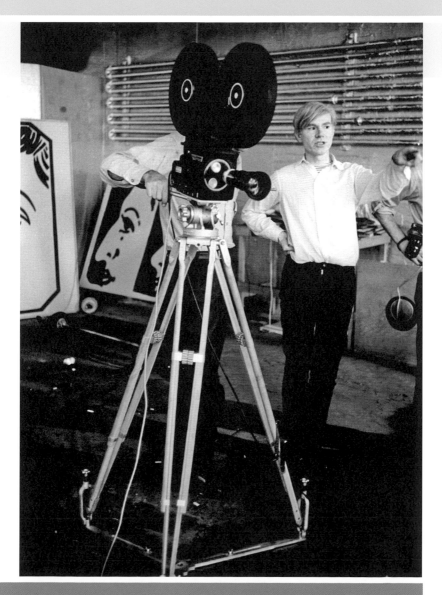

American pop artist Andy Warhol was also known for his
experimental filmmaking in the 1960s.

outside of the mainstream. Typically these films played at colleges, museums, or art-house theaters.

By the 1960s, a lively subculture of artists was making alternative films. These ignored the commercial Hollywood system. The focus was on telling personal stories, exploring issues, or experimenting with artistic formats. Financial success was less important. This movement, called New American Cinema, was influenced by foreign art cinema and documentary techniques.

The growth of film festivals in America helped some of these films find a larger audience. Several cities started film festivals in the 1960s and 1970s. In 1981, actor Robert Redford started the Sundance Film Festival in Utah. It only showed independent features and documentaries. Panels discussed the best regional filmmaking and films by women and minorities. Awards helped support independent filmmakers

Women, Race, and History

Julie Dash directed a historical film about black women on the Sea Islands off the coast of South Carolina and Georgia. *Daughters of the Dust* explores issues of race, gender, sexuality, and family. It debuted at New York's Film Forum and played at the Sundance Film Festival. In 1992, it became the first feature movie by an African-American woman to have a general theatrical release.

from around the world. The festival traveled to other countries, bringing American independent films to those audiences.

Biggest or Best?

Experimental and less expensive films also found opportunities in mainstream cinema. Writer, director, and performer Woody Allen worked from the East Coast, making movies about daily life. His film *Annie Hall* (1977), a romantic comedy that explores the nature of love and relationships, won the Academy Award for Best Picture over *Star Wars*. Critics often consider *Raging Bull* (1980) by director Martin Scorsese and *Blue Velvet* (1986) by director David Lynch among the most important works of the 1980s. *Raging Bull*, a dark story about a prizefighter, was shot in black-and-white with some color sequences. The mystery thriller *Blue Velvet* used garish color and elements of film noir and surrealism.

Some of the most successful films were also controversial. Oliver Stone blended strong characters with a realistic style and symbolism to tackle controversial issues. *Platoon* (1986) was called one of the most realistic fiction films about the Vietnam War.

JFK (1991) started a national debate over the 1963 assassination of President John F. Kennedy. *Thelma and Louise* (1991) by Ridley Scott, with a screenplay by Callie Khouri, turned genre fiction on its head. It shows fugitives on the run from the law, but the criminal heroes are women. It was both praised as a feminist work and criticized for associating women with genre violence.

Hollywood was still largely a male-dominated world, but the 1980s and 1990s saw more women directors. One of the most successful was Penny Marshall, who had hits with *Big* (1988), *Awakenings* (1990), and *A League of Their Own* (1992), which was about professional women baseball players during World War II.

Smoke Signals (1998) was the first film written, directed by, and starring Native Americans, as well as the first Native-American film to receive a commercial release.

African-American filmmakers benefited from the rise of independent filmmaking. Spike Lee was one of the first well-known black directors. His 1986 debut film *She's Gotta Have It* was shot in 12 days on a budget

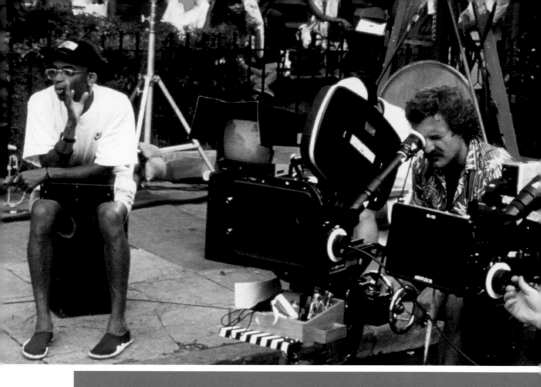

of $175,000, largely provided by grants.[1] The film earned Lee backing from a major studio, and he went on to make popular films that dealt with issues such as racial violence and interracial romance. *Do the Right Thing* (1989), based on a true event, dealt with sudden racial violence with a mix of comedy and tragedy. Lee's biography *Malcolm X* (1992) renewed interest in the civil rights leader from the 1960s. *JFK* and *Malcolm X* showed how historical films could ignite new debate about controversial events. Lee's success proved there was an audience for films about the African-American experience. In 1991, more than a dozen mainstream films by black directors were released. That was more than in the entire decade of the 1980s.

Perhaps the most important role of independent films and film festivals lies in their ability to help more voices be heard. They promote minority and women writers and directors. Women made up a small percentage of the directors with films at Sundance in the 1990s. In 2013, half of the films in the Sundance US Dramatic Competition were directed and written by women.[2]

Indie Goes Mainstream

The term *independent* originally applied to low-budget movies that were not financed or distributed by a large studio. By the mid-1980s, the separate independent film culture was fading. However, larger studios made room for alternative viewpoints and artistic experimentation. The lines between independent films and Hollywood movies blurred.

Alternate or experimental films started gaining more awards recognition and financial success. In 1989, *sex, lies, and videotape* by debut director Steven Soderbergh won awards at Sundance and Cannes. It was then released widely in theaters and became the most successful independent film of its time. Writer and director Quentin Tarantino challenged genre conventions with *Reservoir Dogs* (1992). The crime caper used a fractured narrative and depended more on dialogue than action. He followed up with the wildly successful *Pulp Fiction* (1994). That violent movie earned more than $108 million at the box office, the most of any independent film at the time.[3] It also received seven Academy Award nominations, including Best Picture and Best Director.

In 1997, four of five Best Picture nominees for the Academy Awards were not from large studios: *Fargo*, *The English Patient*, *Secrets & Lies*, and *Shine*.

It was still hard to get studio backing for any movie, but the support of a studio was becoming less necessary. Better and cheaper technology allowed motivated creators to make movies on a relatively small budget. In 1999, *The Blair Witch Project*, by Daniel Myrick and Eduardo Sánchez, debuted at Sundance. The film had been made for $24,000 using inexpensive handheld cameras. It was an independent blockbuster, grossing more than $150 million.[4] The film proved audiences did not need expensive production values to be entertained.

Chapter 9

The Rise of Computers

*I*n the last decades of the 1900s, studios were targeting young people, the ones who would see a movie multiple times and buy tie-in products. Special effects helped attract this group. Computer-generated imagery (CGI) debuted in 1982 with *Tron*, a Disney picture about a human who travels into a computer. In this and other movies of the 1980s, CGI appeared in short scenes that clearly looked like computerized special effects. Then it became possible to transfer film images into a computer, where they could be manipulated digitally. This allowed the Terminator T-1000 to transform from human to liquid metal in James Cameron's *Terminator 2: Judgment Day* (1991).

The special effects in *Tron* were groundbreaking.

Tron **was considered ineligible for the Academy Award for Best Visual Effects because at that time the Academy believed using a computer was unfair.**

CGI woke the film industry with a roar in 1993, with the release of Spielberg's *Jurassic Park*. Clay models of dinosaurs were scanned into a computer. Advanced computer techniques added realistic skin texture and color. The movie's lifelike dinosaurs set box office records worldwide. Only six minutes of the film used CGI, but the technique was blended well with live action and computer work with models. The result set a new standard for visual effects.

CGI found a natural home with animation. Disney had been making both animated and live-action movies, but the company struggled through the 1980s. The studio was revitalized with the 1989 hit *The Little Mermaid* and went on to produce popular and successful films through the 1990s. For many films, Disney continued using hand-drawn animation.

Pixar Animation Studios began as a unit of George Lucas's Lucasfilm but became independent in the

mid-1980s. It then collaborated with Disney on computer-animated features. In 1995, Pixar's *Toy Story* became the first feature-length computer-animated work in film history. The complicated CGI process took a week of work to produce only three and one-half minutes of screen time. But the results were stunning. Director John Lasseter went on to direct *A Bug's Life* (1998), *Toy Story 2* (1999), and *Cars* (2006).

Old-School Animation

CGI did not completely replace other forms of animation. Nick Park began using claymation in short films, releasing his first Wallace and Gromit short in 1990. He went on to direct the feature-length film *The Curse of the Were-Rabbit* (2005) and the short film *A Matter of Loaf and Death* (2008).

Writer, director, and producer Tim Burton had been involved with many movies in the 1980s and 1990s, including *Batman* (1989). In 1993, he used stop-motion animation for the musical *Tim Burton's The Nightmare before Christmas*. After making several more movies with live action or traditional animation, he used stop-motion animation for *The Corpse Bride* in 2005. In *Frankenweenie* (2012), Burton used stop-motion animation, black-and-white imagery, and references to classic monster movies. Despite these old-fashioned elements, it was well received by critics and audiences.

Walt Disney Studios claimed it would make no more 2-D animated films after 2004. All future films would be 3-D, CGI films. However, in 2009, it released *The Princess and the Frog* in traditional 2-D animation. It featured the studio's first ever black female lead.

One trick used in making *The Matrix* was filming in front of a green screen.

The first five feature films Disney and Pixar made together grossed more than $2.5 million worldwide.[1] This gave Pixar the highest average gross revenue per film of any production company. In 2001, an Oscar category was added for Animated Feature Film. Of the next 11 films Pixar released, nine received a nomination. Pixar's *Finding Nemo* (2003) won the Academy Award for Best Animated Feature Film.

CGI appeared in more and more films. Brothers Larry and Andy Wachowski wrote and directed *The Matrix* (1999), which combined the latest special effects techniques. Time-slice photography allowed shots in which an actor appeared to be dodging bullets. To create this effect, technicians used computers to combine film images and still photographs.

CGI could create dramatic scenes without using actual actors or locations, changing the way movies are made. According to critic J. Hoberman, "With the advent of CGI, the history of motion pictures was now, in effect, the history of animation."[2] CGI became common in children's animated movies. It also worked in *Sin City* (2005), which was based on a graphic novel. In the historical epic *300* (2007), only one shot was filmed on location. Everything else was filmed on a soundstage against a green screen. The background was filled in later by computers. CGI was everywhere.

Bigger Effects

Motion-capture technology also brought new possibilities to film. This technique uses computerized cameras to capture an actor's live performance. Digital characters are then developed based on the actor's motion. *The Polar Express* (2004) used the process for a children's film. James Cameron's *Avatar* (2009) advanced the technique with technology that captures facial expressions.

Some critics have felt computers are overused. The Lord of the Rings trilogy (2001, 2002, 2003) used CGI, including motion capture, as a supplement to a large cast, elaborate costumes, and real-world scenery. On the other hand, the Hobbit movies (2012, 2013, 2014) were criticized for an overuse of CGI, which made scenes feel false to some viewers. In a similar vein, *Avatar* and the *Star Wars* prequels (1999, 2002, 2005) were criticized for promoting splashy effects over storytelling. They still succeeded at the box office. That part of the blockbuster formula held true: audiences will come out for big special effects and famous names.

Technology competed to make the film experience better wherever people watched movies. Advances in home entertainment systems—large-screen televisions, high definition pictures, and surround sound—made watching movies at home comparable to going to the theater. Movie theaters had to work harder to lure in customers. How could they make the expensive theater experience better than watching movies at home? As a way to get people back into the

THE BIGGEST BLOCKBUSTER

Perhaps the epitome of the term *blockbuster* is the movie *Titanic*, directed by James Cameron. It was the most expensive movie ever made when it came out in 1997. It cost double its original budget of $100 million.[3] It was also technologically advanced. The film's crew built a 775-foot (236 m) replica of the *Titanic*. Thirteen weeks after its release, *Titanic* was the highest grossing film in North America. It was the first movie ever to earn a billion dollars worldwide.[4] It also won 11 Academy Awards, including Best Picture and Best Director.

theaters, 3-D saw a resurgence. Many movies, both animated and live-action, were released in 3-D in the 2000s. In 2013, 3-D movies made up $1.8 billion of the $10.9 billion from US and Canada box office—more than 16 percent.[5]

Looking Forward

What does the future hold for movies? In many cases, probably more of the same. Hollywood is always seeking a formula that will lead to success. In recent years, that has meant familiar names: adaptations of books and comic books and movies based on cartoons, toys, and amusement park rides. And sequels, sequels, and more sequels. Journalist Mark Harris, writing in 2011, said, "Hollywood has become an institution that is more interested in launching the next rubberized action figure than in making the next interesting movie."[6]

And yet there will be surprises as well. Harris also pondered the surprising success of *Inception* (2010), written and directed by Christopher Nolan. The film features con artists who construct a dreamworld and manipulate it in order to fool their victims. The film had elements of a blockbuster—well-known actors, a respected director, impressive special effects, and a popular genre, the sci-fi action thriller. Yet the plot was complicated and confusing. Much of the action happens in the dreamworld, and the ending is open to multiple interpretations. Many in the business thought it was "too smart" to be a summer hit.[7] However, *Inception* was a popular and critical success. It was nominated for eight Academy Awards and won four, and it made more than $800 million worldwide on a $160 million production budget.[8]

The 2013 science-fiction thriller *Gravity*, by director Alfonso Cuarón, had a similar success. The film features well-known stars and jaw-dropping effects in 3-D. But it broke genre conventions by focusing primarily on two astronauts with no aliens or spaceship battles. It was a financial success, and it was nominated

Still Going to the Theater

People can now choose from hundreds of cable channels, streaming video, and alternative forms of entertainment such as video games. Despite all these options, going to the theater is hardly extinct. In 1990, the United States had more than 23,000 movie screens. In 2010, the number had risen to nearly 40,000.[9] In 2013, more than two-thirds of the population of the United States and Canada went to the movies at least once. Frequent moviegoers, who go to the theater once a month or more, especially helped ticket sales. In 2013, frequent moviegoers bought 50 percent of all movie tickets, though they made up only 11 percent of the population.[10]

In *Gravity*, actress Sandra Bullock took viewers out of this world. Who knows what universes future movies will reveal?

for ten Academy Awards and won seven, including Best Director.

Perhaps audiences are smarter than Hollywood has believed. Audience choices, at the box office and through other methods of watching movies, will determine the future of filmmaking.

TIMELINE

– 1878

Photographer Eadweard Muybridge takes the first successful photographs of an animal in motion.

1882

Frenchman Étienne-Jules Marey invents a camera that can take 12 pictures per second.

1891

Thomas Edison's company unveils the Kinetoscope device.

1892

The first animated cartoons are shown.

1895

Louis and Auguste Lumière patent a movie camera that can both record and project an image to be seen by many people. They demonstrate this in Paris, the first commercial exhibition of projected moving pictures.

1903

Edwin S. Porter produces films such as *The Great Train Robbery*, which develop techniques for telling more complex stories.

1908

The United States has more than 5,000 nickelodeon theaters.

1910s

The star system begins, as previously anonymous stars receive publicity.

1914

The first major studios are thriving in Hollywood, California.

1919

The Homesteader is the first full-length feature film produced by an African American, Oscar Micheaux.

1927

The Jazz Singer, using a system that records sound on discs, is the first "talking" feature-length movie.

1928

Mickey Mouse appears in his first cartoon, *Steamboat Willie*.

TIMELINE CONTINUED

1929
The first Academy Awards are presented.

1934
The first drive-in movie theater opens.

1937
Snow White and the Seven Dwarfs, Disney's first full-length animated feature, is released.

1947
The "Hollywood Ten" are charged with contempt of Congress, and the blacklist is started to keep Communists out of the film business.

1948
Kodak's Eastman film makes color movies less expensive and easier to make.

– 1950s
Musicals, sci-fis, and Westerns are popular during an era of genre filmmaking.

1960s
The New American Cinema movement of independent and underground films is influenced by documentaries and foreign art films.

1975
The first summer blockbuster, *Jaws*, tears through box-office records.

1981
Actor Robert Redford founds the Sundance Film Festival in Park City, Utah.

1982
Computer-generated imagery (CGI) debuts in *Tron*.

1995
Toy Story is the first feature-length computer-animated work in film history.

2000s
More and more films feature CGI technology.

GLOSSARY

art-house theater
A theater that shows foreign films, independent films, or classic movies rather than current mainstream movies.

avant-garde
An experimental artistic style.

blacklist
A list of people under suspicion, who may be boycotted or punished.

blockbuster
A genre defined by a huge budget, a massive advertising campaign, merchandising tie-ins, and other factors designed to bring success.

box office
Literally, the place at a theater where tickets are sold, but also used to refer to the success of a movie in terms of audience size or income from ticket sales.

cult classic
A movie that was not widely successful but becomes beloved by a particular group.

dissolve
A technique in film and video editing where one image gradually fades to another.

documentary
A program that provides a factual report of events.

entrepreneur
A person who takes on financial risk in order to start and manage a business.

film noir

A crime movie characterized by dark lighting, stylized imagery, and complicated morals.

genre

A specific type or category of film, literature, or music, such as comedy or horror.

gross

Total income, before expenses and taxes. For movies, this includes box office plus home entertainment sales and rentals, television rights, and product placement fees.

lens

A light-gathering device in a camera.

phonograph

A machine that uses cylinders or disks to record and play back sound.

propaganda

Information, which may be misleading or biased, used to promote a particular viewpoint or cause.

satire

Humor used to show its subject is weak or ridiculous.

surrealism

An art movement of the 1900s characterized by surprising or dreamlike imagery.

time-lapse

The technique of taking a sequence of images at intervals to record changes that take place slowly, in order to play them back at a faster speed.

ADDITIONAL RESOURCES

Selected Bibliography

Musser, Charles. *Before the Nickelodeon: Edwin S. Porter and the Edison Manufacturing Company*. Berkeley, CA: U of California P, 1991. Print.

Sklar, Robert. *A World History of Film*. New York: Abrams, 2002. Print.

Sklar, Robert. *Movie-Made America: A Cultural History of American Movies*. New York: Vintage, 1994. Print.

Further Readings

Cousins, Mark. *The Story of Film*. London: Pavilion, 2012. Print.

Dzyak, Brian. *What I Really Want to Do on Set in Hollywood: A Guide to Real Jobs in the Film Industry*. Los Angeles: Lone Eagle, 2008. Print.

Thomson, David. *The Big Screen: The Story of the Movies*. New York: Farrar, 2013. Print.

Yager, Fred, Jan Yager, and David Carradine. *Career Opportunities in the Film Industry*. New York: Checkmark, 2009. Print.

Websites

To learn more about Essential Library of Cultural History, visit **booklinks.abdopublishing.com**. These links are routinely monitored and updated to provide the most current information available.

Places to Visit

The Hollywood Museum
1660 North Highland Avenue
Los Angeles, CA 90028
323-464-7776
http://www.thehollywoodmuseum.com
Discover more than 100 years of Hollywood history at this museum, including a large collection of movie memorabilia.

Museum of the Moving Image
36-01 Thirty-Fifth Avenue
Astoria, NY 11106
718-777-6888
http://www.movingimage.us
This museum is the only one in the world focusing on the art, history, and technology of all forms of moving pictures.

SOURCE NOTES

Chapter 1. An American Art Form

None.

Chapter 2. Moving Pictures

1. Charles Musser. *Before the Nickelodeon: Edwin S. Porter and the Edison Manufacturing Company*. Berkeley: U of California P, 1991. Chapter 3. *UC Press E-Books Collection*. Web. 14 Aug. 2014.

2. Ibid. Chapter 4.

Chapter 3. The Birth of Hollywood

1. Brian Manley. "Moving Pictures: The History of Early Cinema." *ProQuest Discovery Guides*. CSA Illumina, July 2011. Web. 14 Aug. 2014. 13.

2. Gordon Reavley. *Social History of the United States: The 1910s*. Santa Barbara, CA: ABC-CLIO, 2009. 324. *Google Book Search*. Web. 14 Aug. 2014.

3. "Reel." *Encyclopaedia Britannica*. Encyclopedia Britannica, 2014. Web.14 Aug. 2014.

4. Robert Sklar. *A World History of Film*. New York: Abrams, 2002. Print. 49.

5. Gerald Baldasty. "The History of Motion Pictures." *University of Washington*. University of Washington, n.d. Web. 14 Aug. 2014.

6. "Mary Pickford." *American Experience*. PBS, 23 July 2004. Web. 14 Aug. 2014.

7. Gerald Baldasty. "The History of Motion Pictures." *University of Washington*. University of Washington, n.d. Web. 14 Aug. 2014.

8. Tim Dirks. "The History of Film: The 1920s." *AMC Filmsite*. American Movie Classics, 2014. Web. 14 Aug. 2014.

9. Michelle Pautz. "The Decline in Average Weekly Cinema Attendance: 1930–2000." *Issues in Political Economy* 11 (2002). *Elon University*. Web. 14 Aug. 2014.

Chapter 4. The Golden Age of Talkies

1. Robert Sklar. *A World History of Film*. New York: Abrams, 2002. Print. 156.

2. Ibid. 168.

3. "History of the Walk of Fame." *Hollywood Walk of Fame*. Hollywood Chamber of Commerce, 2014. Web. 14 Aug. 2014.

4. Robert Sklar. *A World History of Film*. New York: Abrams, 2002. Print. 160.

5. Tim Dicks. "Snow White and the Seven Dwarfs (1937)." *AMC Filmsite Movie Review*. American Movie Classics, n.d. Web. 14 Aug. 2014.

6. Andrew Sarris. *You Ain't Heard Nothin' Yet: The American Talking Film; History & Memory, 1927–1949*. New York: Oxford UP, 1998. Print. 11.

7. Robert Sklar. *Movie-Made America: A Cultural History of American Movies*. New York: Vintage, 1994. Print. 191.

8. Robert Sklar. *A World History of Film*. New York: Abrams, 2002. Print. 92.

Chapter 5. Struggle to Survive

1. "Robert A. Harris's Statement at the Film Preservation Study." *The American Widescreen Museum*. American Widescreen Museum, n.d. Web. 14 Aug. 2014.

2. Robert Sklar. *Movie-Made America: A Cultural History of American Movies*. New York: Vintage, 1994. Print. 250.

3. Ibid. 275.

4. Kerry Seagrave. *American Films Abroad*. Jefferson, NC: McFarland, 1997. 167. *Google Book Search*. Web. 14 Aug. 2014.

5. "Hollywood Ten." *History.com*. A&E Television, 2014. Web. 14 Aug. 2014.

6. Gerald Baldasty. "The History of Motion Pictures." *University of Washington*. University of Washington, n.d. Web. 14 Aug. 2014.

7. Robert Sklar. *A World History of Film*. New York: Abrams, 2002. Print. 314.

8. Tim Dirks. "Animated Films Part 3." *AMC Filmsite*. American Movie Classics, 2014. Web. 14 Aug. 2014.

SOURCE NOTES CONTINUED

Chapter 6. Changing Morals

1. Robert Sklar. *A World History of Film*. New York: Abrams, 2002. Print. 312.

2. Ibid. 382.

3. Barry Monush. "A History of the Oscars." *Paley Center for Media*. Paley Center for Media, 2014. Web. 14 Aug. 2014.

4. Robert Sklar. *A World History of Film*. New York: Abrams, 2002. Print. 312.

5. Ibid. 382.

6. Tim Dirks. "Greatest Box-Office Bombs, Disasters and Film Flops." *AMC Filmsite*. American Movie Classics, 2014. Web. 14 Aug. 2014.

7. Robert Sklar. *A World History of Film*. New York: Abrams, 2002. Print. 382.

Chapter 7. Building the Blockbuster

1. Susan King. "'Jaws' Took a Bite Out of Movie History 35 Years Ago This Week." *Los Angeles Times*. Los Angeles Times, 21 June 2010. Web. 14 Aug. 2014.

2. Robert Sklar. *A World History of Film*. New York: Abrams, 2002. Print. 430.

3. Ibid. 437.

4. "George Lucas." *Biography.com*. A&E Television, 2014. Web. 14 Aug. 2014.

5. "Cable's Story." *NCTA*. National Cable & Telecommunications Association, n.d. Web. 14 Aug. 2014.

6. Tim Dirks. "Timeline of Greatest Film Milestones and Turning Points in Film History: The Year 1992." *AMC Filmsite*. American Movie Classics, 2014. Web. 14 Aug. 2014.

7. Ibid.

8. "30 Years of Sundance Film Festival." *Sundance Institute*. Sundance Institute, 2014. Web. 14 Aug. 2014.

9. "This Day in History: Crouching Tiger, Hidden Dragon Gets 10 Oscar Nominations." *History.com*. A&E Television, 2014. Web. 14 Aug. 2014.

Chapter 8. Independent Films

1. Robert Sklar. *A World History of Film*. New York: Abrams, 2002. Print. 444–445.

2. "30 Years of Sundance Film Festival." *Sundance Institute*. Sundance Institute, 2014. Web. 14 Aug. 2014.

3. "Quentin Tarantino." *Biography.com*. A&E Television, 2014. Web. 14 Aug. 2014.

4. Roger Ebert. "10 Most Influential Films of the Century." *RogerEbert.com*. Ebert Digital, 30 Dec. 1999. Web. 14 Aug. 2014.

Chapter 9. The Rise of Computers

1. Tim Dirks. "Animated Films Part 6." *AMC Filmsite*. American Movie Classics, 2014. Web. 14 Aug. 2014.

2. J. Hoberman. *Film After Film*. London: Verso, 2012. Print. 5.

3. "This Day in History: James Cameron's Titanic Wins 11 Academy Awards." *History.com*. A&E Television, 2014. Web. 14 Aug. 2014.

4. Kevin S. Sandler and Gaylyn Studlar. *Titanic: Anatomy of a Blockbuster*. New Brunswick, NJ: Rutgers UP, 1999. 1. Web. *Google Book Search*. 14 Aug. 2014.

5. "Theatrical Market Statistics 2013." *mpaa.org*. Motion Picture Association of America, n.d. Web. 14 Aug. 2014. 2.

6. Mark Harris. "The Day the Movies Died." *GQ*. Condé Nast, Feb. 2011. Web. 14 Aug. 2014.

7. Ibid.

8. "Inception." *Box Office Mojo*. IMDb, n.d. Web. 14 Aug. 2014.

9. "30 Years of Sundance Film Festival." *Sundance Institute*. Sundance Institute, 2014. Web. 14 Aug. 2014.

10. "Theatrical Market Statistics 2013." *mpaa.org*. Motion Picture Association of America, n.d. Web. 14 Aug. 2014. 2.

INDEX

ABOUT THE AUTHOR

Chris Eboch, aka M. M. Eboch, writes about science, history, and culture for all ages. Her novels for young people include historical fiction, ghost stories, and action-packed adventures.